GW00360039

CHELSEA

A RANDOM HISTORY

An exclusive edition for

This edition first published in Great Britain in 2023 by Allsorted Ltd,
Watford, Herts, UK WD19 4BG

The facts and statistics in this book are correct up to the end of the
2022/23 season. The data comes from publicly available sources and is
presented as correct as far as our knowledge allows. The opinions in this
book are personal and individual and are not affiliated to the football club
in any way. Any views or opinions represented in this book are personal
and belong solely to the book author and do not represent those of
people, institutions or organisations that the football club or publisher
may or may not be associated with in professional or personal capacity,
unless explicitly stated. Any views or opinions are not intended to malign
any religious, ethnic group, club, organisation, company or individual.

© Susanna Geoghegan Gift Publishing
Author: Magnus Allan
Cover design: Milestone Creative
Contents design: Bag of Badgers Ltd
Illustrations: Ludovic Sallé

ISBN: 978-1-915902-09-2

Printed in China

★ CONTENTS ★

Introduction	5
A Quiet day in 1905	8
William Foulke	12
Premier League final positions	14
In the beginning	16
The introduction of ball boys	18
George Hilsdon	20
The Leitch effect	24
Nils Middelboe	26
Half a century with nothing to show	30
Joe Payne	34
The sun came out in Manchester	38
Chelsea's leading all-time goal scorers	40
The mystery of the Chelsea pensioner's hat	42
Ted Drake	44
The Battle of Stamford Bridge (1066)	48
Welcoming the Soviets	50
Respect the badge: pension days	52
Peter Bonetti	54
Respect the badge: Hear us roar	56

The mighty ducklings	59
The 1950s: only the blue's the same	60
Ron Harris	62
We are going to need a bigger bus	66
England caps chart	68
Ray Wilkins	70
The opposition: Leeds United	72
Dennis Wise	76
Ruud Gullit	78
Everything that's wrong with football today	80
Chelsea's top ten first team appearances	86
Gianfranco Zola	88
'Liquidator'	90
The dirtiest match in football	92
Gianluca Vialli	96
Take the Fulham Road until you reach the shed	98
The opposition: Tottenham Hotspur	100
Frank Leboeuf	104
The Battle of Stamford Bridge (2016)	106
Premier League's Top Scorers	110

Raising the roof	112
Claude Makélélé	114
A kick up the 1980s	116
Didier Drogba	118
Respect the badge: a lion in the 1980s/1990s	120
This used to be a football pitch	124
Petr Čech	126
Premier League attendances: Chelsea	128
Fresh investment and new starts	130
Frank Lampard	132
Managers' timeline	136
Chelsea's leading goal scorers by season	138
John Terry	140
The opposition: Arsenal	142
Getting shirty	145
Henry VIII: The Great 'I Am'	148
Chelsea's Premier League goal scorers	152
Chelsea FC Women	154
Karen Carney	156
The Gap	158
The trophy cabinet	160

"I CAME TO CHELSEA
AND IT WAS 'OH, YOU
CAN'T PLAY CHAMPIONS
LEAGUE, YOU CAN'T DO
THIS, YOU CAN'T DO
THAT' AND I PROVED
THEM WRONG."

Gary Cahill.

★ INTRODUCTION: ★

120 YEARS OF HIGHS AND LOWS

When times are good, Chelsea have delivered scintillating football, bringing stars from all over the world to west London to delight fans. Somehow though, crisis is never too far away, and the team have regularly found themselves mired in difficulties.

Part of the reason for this is that one of the team's greatest assets is also its biggest curse. Formed in west London to make the most of the burgeoning football culture at the turn of the 20th century, Chelsea could rely on fantastic gate receipts from day one.

But they are also hemmed in by the massive pressure on space in populous west London. While other teams have moved around seemingly on a whim, building new stadiums to ensure swanky match-day experiences, Chelsea have been penned into Stamford Bridge, which has left them facing all kinds of issues with redevelopment. Stamford Bridge is an institution that has witnessed many a titanic football struggle, but thanks to population density and, weirdly, King Henry VIII (kid you not – see page 148) redeveloping it is also a titanically expensive struggle.

Another of Chelsea's greatest assets is character, both on and off the pitch. Chelsea's west London home has also made it a magnet for the great and the good, with a glittering list of stars holding season tickets and bringing their celebrity friends to the club when they are in the country. Sir Michael Caine, Damon Albarn, Bill Clinton and, of course, Lord Richard Attenborough have watched matches at Stamford Bridge, as have Jimmy Page, Gordon Ramsay and David Mellor.

When Chelsea are at their best, the team brings the world to Stamford Bridge, uniting ultra-fans, politicians, musicians and all manner of other celebrities. What the club has achieved so well over the last few years has been bringing all of these constituencies together, offering exceptional football that makes going to Stamford Bridge a night to remember.

Character also shines out when you look through the list of names of people who have played for this club. There's grit behind the smile that undermines their reputation as west London dandies, whether you are thinking about William Foulke (see page 12), who thought nothing of picking up opposition forwards and throwing them into his goal if they thought they were good enough to try to get one past him, or Chopper Harris, a man with a fearsome reputation who didn't actually receive a red card during the whole of his career (see page 62).

It's been a tough road so far and Chelsea have often found themselves on the brink of catastrophe, but the club has learned through adversity and has a glittering future ahead. For the last two decades, Chelsea have been one of the best clubs in the world, and there's no reason why it shouldn't stay that way in the future.

★ A QUIET DAY IN 1905 ★

Tottenham was formed by a bunch of cricket-playing kids who decided that they wanted to form an association football team so that they had a ball to chase during the winter months. Arsenal was formed by a bunch of blokes with impressive moustaches deciding that they wanted to form a team based around the munitions factory where they worked. Both of these events happened in the 1880s.

Chelsea was formed a quarter of a century later because literally nobody could bring themselves to watch Fulham anymore. This is, of course, untrue. Although they really were formed in 1905.

What actually happened is that a businessman with the most Victorian of names ever, Henry Augustus Mears, known affectionately as 'Gus', bought the Stamford Bridge athletics ground and an adjoining market garden (basically an allotment that helped feed city dwellers back in the day). He wanted to build one of the world's greatest football stadiums on the land, and discussed moving Fulham FC there with its chairman Henry Norris, who was later chairman of Arsenal – because things were convoluted at the dawn of football.

He didn't get Norris' support; instead, Gus decided to bring some of his west London associates together and form a football club of his own, developing the Stamford Bridge athletics ground as their home.

Gus' associates were a well-to-do bunch, which is not that surprising given the demographic of Chelsea even then. What this meant was that rather than growing slowly, earning a reputation by scrapping in the Sunday leagues on mud-heavy recreation grounds in front of three spectators and a dog, Chelsea went pretty quickly from an interesting idea to a fully fledged professional football club in around 12 months. It was 1905 and they put out a press release announcing their creation. They were not mucking about.

It's worth noting that up until that point, while professional football had taken off in the Midlands and the north, there hadn't been a

London team in the First Division until Woolwich Arsenal had finally joined the big leagues in 1903/04. Attendances at the FA Cup final, though, often held at nearby Crystal Palace, regularly reached 60,000 people, so there was clearly an appetite in London for the professional game. From a standing start, Chelsea wanted to catapult themselves into becoming one of the most important teams in the south.

There were several reasons for the ambition, such as the first board of Chelsea including a prominent local pub landlord who was very keen to bring the game to the borough to set the tills ringing on a Saturday afternoon. One of the members had built and owned the Dell in Southampton, so brought considerable experience to the board.

There were less than three months between the first meeting of the club's board at an upstairs room in the Rising Sun pub (now the Butcher's Hook if you are in west London and want to have a gander) and its election to the Second Division of the Football League – and they'd done it without a ball being kicked. By the end of the 1906/07 season, Chelsea had made it to the First Division.

"EVERY TIME HE WENT FOR HIS POCKET AND YOU THOUGHT HE WAS GOING TO BOOK SOMEBODY, HE PULLED OUT HIS HANKY, BLEW HIS NOSE AND SAID, 'GET ON WITH IT, WILL YOU?'"

Chelsea defender David Webb reflects on the laissez-faire approach to refereeing in the 1970 FA Cup final.

★ WILLIAM FOULKE ★

Look at any photo of Chelsea's earliest team and hulking over the top of all the other players will be William Foulke. Foulke, who was 193 cm tall (6 foot 4 inches for those who haven't caught up with metric measures) and weighed up to 152 kilograms (24 stone), signed from Sheffield United for £50.

He'd won the FA Cup twice (in 1898/99 and 1901/02) and the First Division (in 1897/98) with the Blades, and he captained Chelsea in the early days. Foulke played 35 games in his single season with Chelsea, letting in just 28 goals, while 17 goals went in during the six games he missed, suggesting that while his size made him a novelty, he was also a useful addition to the team (or that no one had thought of back-up keepers).

Naturally, in those less sensitive days, he was popularly known as 'Fatty Foulke'. This could be why he became increasingly temperamental and as famous for his antics as his skill. He was said to feel quite entitled to walk off the pitch if he decided that his defenders weren't putting in enough effort. There were also stories of him arriving early for breakfast before the rest of the team and eating every single plate of food before his team mates showed up. His on- and off-field antics made him very popular with the crowds.

13

· CHELSEA ·

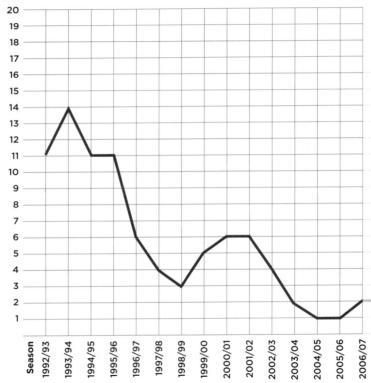

Position

Season

PREMIER LEAGUE
★ FINAL POSITIONS ★

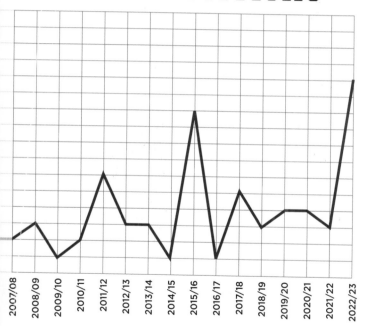

★ IN THE BEGINNING ... ★

In the beginning, there was an athletics track, and the track was oval. This meant that there was a healthy space in the middle where people could do things other than running fast, such as throwing stuff of various weights over distances and jumping over higher and higher things. There was talk of an association football club being set up in the 1890s, but nothing came of it.

The space in the middle of the Stamford Bridge athletics track did get used for the 1898 shinty World Championship. Shinty, which is a bit like field hockey with more broken noses, is a game played predominantly in the highlands of Scotland, so presumably the shinty World Championship was a bit like American baseball's World Series – except with even fewer countries involved. To be fair, one of the shinty teams involved in the World Championship was London-based, and the game has been played at several football stadiums down the years, including Old Trafford.

When it came to constructing the stadium, Mears and

his team turned to specialist football ground architect Archibald Leitch, who was basically Great Britain's go-to stadium designer between 1899 and 1939 (see page 22). He created the East Stand and built up the other three sides using earth excavated from the development of the Piccadilly tube line. Chelsea started out with a stadium that could welcome 100,000 people on match day.

Chelsea Football Club was developed to entertain the people of west London, but it was also created by some fairly hard-nosed business folk, so the fact that the stadium had such a large capacity meant that the tills would be ringing a healthy tune. The bottom line is that within two years of formation, 50,000–60,000 people were making their way to Stamford Bridge on match days, while Woolwich Arsenal, at the time playing in a relatively sparsely populated region south of the river Thames, were lucky if they could get a third of that number through the turnstiles.

Football's a form of entertainment, but football clubs need to at least break even. Chelsea were on to a good thing right from the get-go.

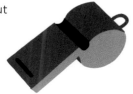

THE INTRODUCTION OF
★ BALL BOYS ★

The game as we know it today didn't arrive fully formed in 1863, after which the Football Association (FA) codified the rules of football. The basics were there, but some things that we now take for granted took time to be developed.

Ball boys, one of the most logical things for a match to have if you want to keep things flowing, didn't arrive on the scene until 1905 – and it was Chelsea that first employed them. When they were first deployed, though, they were only there to help the goalie.

Chelsea signed William Foulke (see page 12) from Sheffield United for their first season in 1905. He was a big chap, and the management at the time thought they could accentuate his size by having two children stand on either side of the goal (this was the early Edwardian era – be glad they weren't being forced up chimneys). These little fellas would sometimes very kindly run and get the ball if it

18

missed the goal to save Foulke a bit of energy, which was particularly important at a ground like Chelsea's, where the running track meant that the space behind the goal was quite large.

Someone, somewhere, thought this was something that would be useful to have at every game, and they quickly became a feature of the sport.

Ball boys tend to be made up of academy players, and, as a result, several ball boys have ended up becoming professionals, including Callum Hudson-Odoi, Mateo Kovačić and Álvaro Morata. Even Peter Crouch was a ball boy at Stamford Bridge once upon a time.

★ GEORGE HILSDON ★

George Hilsdon was a prolific goal scorer who started playing in the 1903/04 season for West Ham United before moving across London to join Chelsea in 1906, attracted by a wage that was said to be £4 per week. Known in those pre-politically correct times as 'Gatling Gun George', because of the speed and regularity of his shots on goal, he scored 108 goals in 164 games for the Pensioners (as they were known then), including a five-goal haul on his debut.

Delivering 27 goals in his first season for Chelsea helped the team earn promotion to the First Division, and Hilsdon became the joint highest scorer in Chelsea's inaugural year in the top flight, delivering 26 league goals. He also scored 14 goals in eight appearances for England.

Despite his prolific scoring record, Hilsdon is said to have been one of those that enjoyed the nightlife a little too much, so he was released in 1912, finding his way back to West Ham, then plying their trade in the Southern League First Division, where he became the Hammers' top scorer in the 1912/13 season.

He fell on hard times and was eventually buried in an unmarked grave in Leicestershire in 1941, but Chelsea supporters crowdfunded a headstone that was put up for him in 2015.

Hilsdon is also commemorated at Stamford Bridge by a weathervane that presides over the East Stand. It is said that if it is ever taken down, the consequences for Chelsea would be dire. While this kind of talk should generally be met with a raised eyebrow, it's worth noting that when the weathervane was taken down for renovation in the 1970s, Chelsea struggled financially and found themselves relegated. If Stamford Bridge is redeveloped, it might be worth thinking about finding a way to keep it in place.

He remains the club's 10th highest scorer.

His son, meanwhile, rose to become a committed bit-part actor and can often be seen in the backgrounds of British films in the 1960s to the 1980s, including several *Carry On …* films, a couple of Hammer horrors and, superbly, a breakout role as a newspaper seller in *An American Werewolf in London*. He also played the father of private detective Hazell in the TV adaptation of a popular 1970s book series that was co-authored by none other than Chelsea midfielder and future England manager Terry Venables (writing as P.B. Yuill). Insert shrug emoji.

"I DON'T KNOW WHERE HORSE RIDING COULD HAVE TAKEN ME, AND IT'S SOMETHING I CAN ALWAYS GO BACK TO WHEN I'VE RETIRED FROM FOOTBALL, BUT THE CROSSROADS CAME IN MY LIFE WHEN CHELSEA WANTED TO SIGN ME AND MAKE ME A PROFESSIONAL FOOTBALLER IN 2013 WHEN I WAS 20."

Millie Bright.

★ THE LEITCH EFFECT ★

At first glance, it's easy to be a bit sniffy about Chelsea turning to Archibald Leitch to design Stamford Bridge, given that he was also involved in the design of Craven Cottage, Highbury and White Hart Lane.

Chelsea are a unique club, so surely their status, ambition and depth of pocket deserved a dedicated stadium designer? And then you look at the list of other teams that Leitch delivered stadiums and stands for between 1899 and his death in 1939 ...

- Arsenal
- Aston Villa
- Blackburn Rovers
- Bradford City
- Charlton
- Crystal Palace
- Derby County
- Dundee
- Everton
- Fulham
- Hamilton Academical
- Hearts
- Huddersfield Town
- Kilmarnock
- Leicester City
- Liverpool
- Manchester United
- Middlesbrough

- Millwall
- Newcastle United
- Plymouth
- Portsmouth
- Preston North End
- Queen's Park
- Rangers
- Sheffield United
- Sheffield Wednesday
- Southampton
- Sunderland
- Tottenham Hotspur
- West Ham United
- Wolverhampton Wanderers

... as well as several cricket, rugby and even Gaelic football stands. He also started work on Manchester City's stadium, but this was interrupted by the outbreak of World War I and was ultimately put on hold.

Early in his career as a stadium designer, a stand that he designed at Ibrox collapsed, killing several people. He developed a new way of strengthening the stadium for the rebuild, which enhanced his reputation and let him build a monopoly.

Frankly, he was a busy bloke who knew what he was doing.

★ NILS MIDDELBOE ★

Chelsea have always been forward-looking and ambitious, bringing in talent when they found it. This went as far as being the first team in England to attract overseas talent.

In 1913, the team was joined by Nils Middelboe – a Danish amateur footballer and track and field athlete – by all accounts, securing his signature despite strong interest from Newcastle United.

Middelboe had represented Denmark at the 1908 and 1912 Olympic Games, winning silver medals for football both times (Great Britain took both golds). He held the honour of scoring his national team's first Olympic goal. Playing with Kjøbenhavns Boldklub (KB), a precursor of Copenhagen FC, he'd also won the Danish KBU, an amateur league, five times between 1904 and 1913, and he was also a Danish triple jump and 4 × 100 metres relay champion, setting Danish records in the 800 metres and triple jump.

When he reached London, he kept himself busy, dividing his time between playing for Chelsea as an amateur while earning a crust working at a bank (he was a fully qualified lawyer). His work meant that he struggled to get the time off to travel north on a Friday afternoon with the rest of the team (this was 50 years before someone got around to building the M1, so nipping oop north to wherever on the morning of the match wasn't really an option). As a result, he only played 12 away matches in the decade that he spent with the club.

He could have played more and earned more by signing on with Chelsea professionally, but, by his own admission, he wasn't really into football all that much.

He was 6 foot 2 inches (188 cm) in his football socks, making him statuesque by the standards of the day. The media didn't take long to start calling him 'the Great Dane' – because they are nothing if not imaginative.

He made 175 appearances for Chelsea between 1913 and 1923 and continued to be involved with football after he moved on, both in England and then back home in Denmark. He even steered KB to another title in 1940.

"YOU CAN CALL
ME ANYTHING, BUT
DON'T CALL ME LATE
FOR DINNER."

William 'Fatty' Foulke

HALF A CENTURY WITH NOTHING ★ TO SHOW ★

Chelsea arrived relatively late on the football scene, but they came, as they say, from money. The Chelsea area of west London had been affluent since the city began to grow, and the football club was set up and supported by a group of wealthy, experienced benefactors.

The club was able to hold its own in the Edwardian transfer market as soon as it was formed, and was well known for sending scouts all over the British Isles to try to attract all the best talent. Right from the off, Chelsea was able to attract 40,000 people through the turnstiles at Stamford Bridge, which made it that rarest of things: a profitable football club.

In some ways, though, Chelsea's affluence worked against it in those early days. There was always a temptation for the club to throw money at a problem on or off the pitch, but often they might have been better spending a bit more time moulding great talent into a great team. Looking back through some of the historical bios, it's interesting to see how often it seems that talent came to west London and found itself distracted by the bright lights and entertainments on offer in the capital.

Chelsea made it to the First Division in 1907/08 season, for their third season. This was an ambitious team with professionalism at its core. They had the grounds, they had the resources. Of course, it was going to take time to bed into the top flight, but this was Chelsea, nothing would stand in their way.

They came 13th in their debut season in the First Division, 11th in their second and then found themselves relegated. In 1910/11 they came third in the Second Division, and then enjoyed promotion with a second place the year after. They came 18th, one place (although five points) clear of relegation in 1912/13, a creditable eighth the next season, but 19th the year after as the Football League was put on hiatus for the duration of World War I. They would have been relegated were it not for a sympathy vote they received following some shenanigans in the north-west that are probably best glossed over to spare other people's blushes (Basically, two teams that play in the north west and wear red were allegedly caught in a match fixing scandal that caused no end of ill feeling in north London. Chelsea were only tangentially involved so it doesn't need to take up our time here).

The pattern continued during the interwar period, with the team spending most of the 1920s in the Second Division before climbing back up in second place in the 1929/30 season and delivering an average First Division position of 14th during the 1930s. The team had plenty of fans, but they weren't really offering much to cheer about, other than good individual skills.

There was also the slight impression that Stamford Bridge was more about generating revenue than winning football trophies. There was a speedway team that operated from the football ground, there was greyhound racing and a variety of other activities that provided revenue – but potentially took some of the focus away from the football.

On the pitch, they had become something like the Harlem Globetrotters basketball exhibition team – chock-full of talent, full of tricks, but not able to play the game competitively or consistently.

As the world recovered from the horrors of World War II, the leadership team at Chelsea realised that they simply could not go back to the way things were. Something had to be done.

THE FIRST EUROPEAN CHAMPIONSHIP WAS HELD IN THE 1955/56 SEASON, BUT UNDER PRESSURE FROM THE ENGLISH FOOTBALL ASSOCIATION, CHELSEA DECLINED THE OPPORTUNITY TO PARTICIPATE.

★ JOE PAYNE ★

Joe Payne was known as 'Ten-goal Joe Payne' on account of him scoring 10 goals in a match for Luton Town against Bristol Rovers in 1936 (which finished 12–0). It was an achievement that earned him a £2 bonus on top of his £4 per week wage. The funny thing is that up to that point he had been played as a centre half and was only filling in at centre forward because the Hatters were suffering an injury crisis up front. His name wasn't even in the match-day programme because he wasn't actually expected to play.

Payne didn't score for the first 23 minutes so a decent proportion of the Luton crowd will have been tutting and muttering something about the manager not having a clue. But by half-time he had the first of three hat-tricks, and the game finished with him officially scoring nine goals, equalling the existing Football League record. After the match, the referee changed his opinion about one of the goals scored by a teammate and awarded it to Payne (claiming that the other player had struck it after it had crossed the goal line). With no video assistance referee (VAR), action replays or, let's face it, actual match footage, it's impossible to argue, and so Payne has gone down in the history books and holds the record for the most goals scored in an English Football League match – a record that still stands today.

As you might expect, Payne stayed up front for the next season, knocking in 55 goals in 39 matches (still a club record) and helping Luton become champions of the Third Division South.

The next year, he was signed for Chelsea for a healthy fee, and while he started brightly enough, slotting in 21 goals in 36 appearances, World War II interrupted his, and many other, careers. After the war and a bout of ill health, he signed for West Ham United.

Payne played for England once, scoring twice in an 8-0 demolition of Finland. *Anteeksi*, lads.

CHELSEA ARE THE ONLY CLUB TO APPOINT THREE PLAYER-MANAGERS IN A ROW (GLENN HODDLE, RUUD GULLIT AND GIANLUCA VIALLI).

"CHELSEA GAVE ME WHAT I WAS LOOKING FOR WHEN I LEFT LIVERPOOL: TROPHIES. I'LL ALWAYS SEE IT AS A SUCCESS."

Fernando Torres.

THE SUN CAME OUT
★ IN MANCHESTER ... ★

A couple of decades after launching with great fanfare, Chelsea had become a byword for high-spending entertainment that never really challenged for trophies or titles. It got to the point that popular 1920s and 1930s light entertainer Norman Long ('A song, a smile and a piano', which, let's face it, would be quite a good strapline for a sinister horror movie) was winning popular acclaim with the song 'On the Day that Chelsea Won the Cup'.

In it, he explained that he had a dream where the world was turned upside down on the day that Chelsea won the cup. Landlords came around to do the repairs on their tenant's houses, film stars had the same wife that they'd had the day before and, most ridiculously, the sun came out in Manchester. Imagine that.

Every generation has its TikTok equivalents, and a few of them will still be funny 10 years later, but the fact that

Chelsea had failed to deliver was seriously starting to become a problem for the club. They were also burning through the cash, offering glittering football that didn't translate to silverware.

Now a little while ago I dreamed the most amazing dream,
It tickled me to death when I woke up.
Now you know just how impossible the things we dream of are,
But I dreamt that Chelsea went and won the Cup.
Of course, as the result of an astounding thing like this,
A host of other strange events occurred.
All folks and things were opposite to what they really are,
And the happenings were really most absurd ...

On the day that Chelsea went and won the final
All the universe went off the reel.
Great Sir Harry Lauder used a five bob postal order
To stop his shoe from rubbing at the heel.
The sun came out in Manchester and funny things like that
Jack Jones MP played golf and wore a kilt and Winston's hat.
And a pigeon hatched a Guinea pig and blamed it on the cat
On the day that Chelsea went and won the cup ...

There are three more verses, but you get the idea.

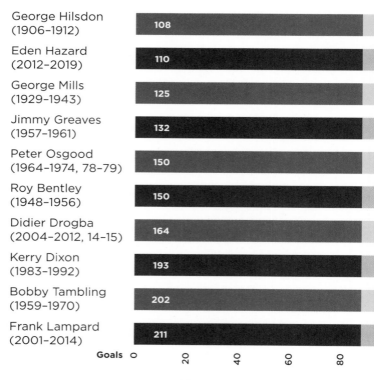

George Hilsdon (1906–1912) — 108
Eden Hazard (2012–2019) — 110
George Mills (1929–1943) — 125
Jimmy Greaves (1957–1961) — 132
Peter Osgood (1964–1974, 78–79) — 150
Roy Bentley (1948–1956) — 150
Didier Drogba (2004–2012, 14–15) — 164
Kerry Dixon (1983–1992) — 193
Bobby Tambling (1959–1970) — 202
Frank Lampard (2001–2014) — 211

Goals 0 20 40 60 80

CHELSEA'S LEADING ALL-TIME GOAL ★ SCORERS ★

(ALL COMPETITIONS)

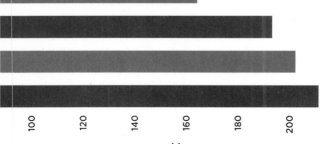

100   120   140   160   180   200   220

THE MYSTERY OF THE CHELSEA ★ PENSIONER'S HAT ★

There are many odd things about the early days of football. It was a chaotic time, no one really expected football to still be important over a century later and, as a result, they didn't think to leave much information. There are many mysteries that will probably only ever be solved by either very serious academics or intergalactic wanderers that mooch about time and space in magical blue boxes powered by charisma and incomprehensible storylines. One of these mysteries involves Chelsea's first badge.

Chelsea Pensioners have two uniforms. The scarlet one that they wear when they are out and about or attending ceremonial events, and the blue one that they are encouraged to wear when they are back home at Chelsea Royal Hospital.

Chelsea Football Club's badge that served for the best part of half a century featured a Chelsea Pensioner in his (and it was 'his' because the first female veterans were not admitted until 2009) scarlet dress coat, but the weird thing is that he wasn't wearing the ceremonial tricorne (three-pointed) hat that the pensioners are supposed to wear with the scarlet uniform. He's wearing a shako, the peaked military cap that was introduced in 1843 and is supposed to be matched with the blue uniform.

Knowing how touchy the people of His Majesty's Armed Forces tend to be about uniforms and making sure that everyone's got the right regimental stripes in the right place when they are represented on stage and screen, it seems odd that this was allowed to slide for the first half century of Chelsea's existence.

It's possible that the Chelsea Pensioners have served their country and most have achieved an advanced age, so the authorities and other assorted pedants don't enforce the tricorne hat at non-ceremonial events. It could also be that the pensioner portrayed on the badge saw Stamford Bridge as an extension of his home. It could also be that in 1905 someone at Stamford Bridge thought that drawing a peaked cap was significantly easier than drawing a tricorne hat. We may never know.

★ TED DRAKE ★

Ted Drake had won the League with Arsenal in 1934/5 (with 42 goals in 41 league appearances), and in 1935/36 he achieved acclaim by tucking all seven away in a 7–1 victory at Aston Villa. He also won the 1935/36 FA Cup and lifted the League trophy again in 1937/38.

To put it bluntly, he had enjoyed success.

Once his playing days were behind him, he'd become a manager, first at Hendon then at Reading, where he had taken the Royals to second in the Third Division South in both 1948/49 and 1951/52 (although only the champions were promoted at the time).

He was clearly ambitious.

He also fitted the spirit of Chelsea, presenting himself in public in sharp suits, a swagger and slick-backed hair held in place, in all likelihood, with a generous application of Brylcreem.

In other words, he looked the part.

Drake joined Chelsea as manager for the start of the 1952/53 season, promising to build a spirit into the team that would bring results that matched the club's ambitions.

Breaking with tradition, he used his knowledge of football further down the leagues to make some shrewd signings, bringing players to Chelsea before they had become superstars, rather than bringing in players who were already stars and might, as a result, be more difficult to manage.

Within three years, Drake had delivered the First Division title to Stamford Bridge, making him the first person in English football to win the League as both a player and a manager. The inaugural Charity Shield followed three months later. After that though, despite bringing a promising crop of youngsters into the team (see page 59), there were no more major successes for Chelsea, and Drake moved on early in the 1961/62 season.

He subsequently became part of the management team at Fulham and then Barcelona, but that shouldn't be held against him; this was the man that delivered Chelsea's first League and Cup success.

"[THERE IS] NOT MUCH DIFFERENCE IN CLASS THROUGHOUT MOST OF THE FIRST DIVISION TEAMS. THE TEAMS WHICH WIN SUCCESS ARE THE TEAMS WHICH WORK HARD AT THE GAME, AND FIGHT ON AND HOLD ON WHEN THE LITTLE EXTRA EFFORT IS NEEDED. ONLY HIGH CLUB SPIRIT PRODUCES THIS BURST."

Ted Drake knew that team spirit is what gets you over the line.

THE BATTLE OF STAMFORD BRIDGE ★ (1066) ★

It's a small thing, but it's worth mentioning because generations of schoolchildren across Britain have had their hearts broken by a simple misunderstanding when the teacher says that they are going to study the Battle of Stamford Bridge in the next lesson. The Battle of Stamford Bridge in 1066 did not take place in west London.

Without going too far down a GCSE history rabbit hole, the Battle of Stamford Bridge took place in east Yorkshire and was a mighty coming together of two armies: one led by the English King Harold Godwinson; the other by the Norwegian King Harald Hardrada, who had chummed up with the English king's brother, Tostig Godwinson, because back in those days when royal families went to war, they really went to war.

The reason for the confusion is that Stamford in old English means 'sandy ford' or 'crossing' – basically a place where it was relatively easy to get across a river. It was also a good place to build a bridge. And in a world of simple maps and limited imaginations, people tended to call things what they were. So, in old England, there were actually quite a lot of Stamford Bridges. For example, one in west London, where there's now a football club, and another in east Yorkshire, where there was a battle just under 1,000 years ago.

Unless the teacher in question is straying quite significantly from the National Curriculum, they are unlikely to be talking about the infamous match between Chelsea and Tottenham in 2016 (see page 106), which has been dubbed 'the Battle of Stamford Bridge'. If they are talking about the infamous match between Chelsea and Tottenham in 2016, then fair play to them; it was a cracking match (unless you are a Spurs fan).

WELCOMING
★ THE SOVIETS ★

Less than three months after the end of World War II, Stamford Bridge hosted a friendly match with Dynamo Moscow, then League Champions of the Soviet Union, as part of a tour of Great Britain. With competitive football suspended for the previous six years, the match in Chelsea became one of the hottest tickets in town, and while official attendance figures say that there were around 75,000 spectators, estimates suggest that the actual crowd was around 100,000 strong. Residents in the area were said to be hiring out their front gardens so people had somewhere to put their bikes (there's an idea for an app). Several fans climbed on to the roof of the East Stand (with one tumbling to his death).

It's said that touts were able to sell 10-shilling (50p) tickets for £5, and there were so many people in the stadium that they were standing over the running track right up to the edge of the pitch. One Moscow goal was disallowed because it was judged to have gone in off a spectator (hard to know what VAR would have made of that).

The assembled masses were bemused by the Soviets coming on to the pitch 15 minutes early and warming up with some training drills rather than having the more traditional pre-match ciggy, but after the match, several of the Chelsea players marvelled at the team's speed and ability to pass and move.

The game ended with three goals apiece, although, in the interests of peace, some historians have suggested that the referee allowed a clearly offside goal from the Russian team to stand. Others disagree, suggesting that the ball came off a Chelsea player and, as a result, put the Moscow attack onside.

It was a game that had everything: diplomacy, six goals and an offside controversy that people are still debating 80 years later.

RESPECT THE BADGE:
★ PENSION DAYS ★

Chelsea's original badge paid respect to a feature of the borough that the team called home. The scarlet-coated Chelsea Pensioners had been part of the weft and weave of life in west London since King Charles II started work on a hospital to treat army veterans in the 1680s, and the dress-uniform that they are entitled to wear when they are out and about adds a vibrancy to the streets, particularly when they are out in force.

As a result, Chelsea FC's first badge featured a profile portrait of a Chelsea Pensioner with the words 'Chelsea Football Club' written in a circle around it, and the team itself was initially known as 'the Pensioners'.

By the time the 1950s rolled around, Chelsea had gone nearly half a century without winning any silverware; a fact that had made them a bit of a laughing stock. With the club looking for a way to redefine itself and bring the promise of excitement on a Saturday afternoon, it was decided that it was time for a new image.

They changed their nickname to 'the Blues' and retired the pensioner from their badge in 1952, replacing it initially with a stylised 'CFC' as an emblem that lasted for a single season, before alighting on the lion as the centrepiece of the badge that has survived in one form or another to this day.

The association between the club and the Chelsea Pensioners has continued, however. Many of the club's shirts have had scarlet detailing or trim that is the same colour as the Chelsea Pensioners' dress uniforms. In recognition of their shared history, the Chelsea Pensioners formed a guard of honour for the Premier League-winning team in 2004/05 and again in 2009/10.

★ PETER BONETTI ★

Peter 'The Cat' Bonetti played in 600 domestic league games for Chelsea, making 729 appearances in all competitions. He started in 1959, joining Drake's Ducklings after his mum wrote in and requested a trial for her son, and had a second stint with the club that ended in 1979. He kept 208 clean sheets for the Blues, a record that stood until Petr Čech surpassed it in 2014.

During his time with Chelsea, Bonetti won the FA Youth Cup in 1960, the League Cup in 1965, the FA Cup in 1969/70 and the UEFA Cup Winners' Cup in 1971.

He only played for England seven times (his career ran parallel to the mighty Gordon Banks), but was part of the victorious 1966 World Cup squad, finally receiving his winner's medal in 2009 after a long campaign to have the entire squad recognised, rather than just the players on the pitch.

Later in his career he played for Dundee and Woking, before retiring to the Isle of Mull where he worked as a postman.

RESPECT THE BADGE: ★ HEAR US ROAR ★

While Chelsea was trying to update its image and turbo-charge its reputation in the 1950s, it looked to its heritage for its new crest, specifically the coat of arms of the Metropolitan Borough of Chelsea, a predecessor of today's Royal Borough of Kensington and Chelsea.

In heraldic terms, there is a whole language (above and beyond the copious amounts of Latin and courtly French) devoted to what a lion on a courtly shield or crest is doing. If it was standing with its hindleg together on the ground and its forelegs together in the air, it would be a 'lion salient'; if it had all four paws on the floor and looked like it was waiting for a treat like a good boy, it would be a 'lion sejant' (you did ask). A lion lying down with its eyes closed is, of course, a 'lion dormant'.

A 'lion rampant regardant' is a posh way of saying that it's a lion standing on two legs with its forepaws raised looking over its shoulder with its tail up, paws in striking position. This is said, by the people who decide these things, to symbolise courage, royalty and valour, making it an appropriate symbol for Chelsea Football Club. So that's what was put on the rechristened Blues' shirts in the 1950s.

The lion rampant regardant, which is associated with Earl Cadogan, aka Viscount Chelsea, was incorporated into the coat of arms of the Metropolitan Borough of Chelsea, which also features a staff down the middle (technically known as a crozier, but you can go down that particular rabbit hole in your own time). Chelsea FC's lion proudly holds the staff aloft. Which is just as well because he could have someone's eye out with those claws, particularly given that he isn't looking where he's going.

The other animals that featured on the Metropolitan Borough of Chelsea's coat of arms were a stag (presumably rejected by Chelsea for its association with nearby Richmond), a pair of boars (presumably rejected because you don't want to risk going from being known as 'the Pensioners' to being known as 'the Boars') and a winged bull (presumably rejected because, at the time, it was beginning to feel like Chelsea's pursuit of success was deeply mythical).

Either way, the lion rampant holding a crozier worked well and became a badge that the Chelsea faithful could get behind. And for the next 30 years it was central to the club's identity.

AT ONE POINT, CHELSEA HELD BOTH THE CHAMPIONS LEAGUE AND THE EUROPA LEAGUE TITLES, THE FIRST TEAM TO DO THIS. IT WAS ONLY FOR 10 DAYS, BUT IT MADE FOR AN IMPRESSIVE TROPHY CABINET.

THE MIGHTY
★ DUCKLINGS ★

The Chelsea Juniors had been set up in the late 1930s, under the management of William 'Billy' Birrell, but the war understandably slowed its development. As the 1950s got underway, though, it became increasingly clear that this was a useful, low-cost resource for the rechristened Blues, particularly as the team tried to move away from the high cost/low success recruitment policy of bringing in established stars and giving them the run of the place.

Over the next few years, these bright young things, known as 'Drake's Ducklings', included such future luminaries as Peter Bonetti (see page 54), Peter Brabrook, Barry Bridges, Jimmy Greaves, Ken Shellito, Bobby Tambling and Terry Venables.

While there wasn't any further success for the first team for the rest of Drake's tenure, Chelsea Juniors delivered the FA Youth Cup in 1959/60 and again in 1960/61.

THE 1950S: ONLY THE
★ BLUE'S THE SAME ★

Drake led what could probably be described as a long overdue revolution at Chelsea. Out went the old guard, and with them went the bottomless pockets that had provided Chelsea with a string of shining stars that were, perhaps, more often than not in the process of falling to earth.

The badge changed, the nickname changed, the training regime changed. One of the few things that didn't change during the decade was that the club kept playing in royal blue.

In Drake's analysis, there was very little that separated the top teams in the First Division from the rest of the teams; they all had the talent, they had the skill, but what they didn't all have was the hunger – the appetite to win. To go the extra mile and pull a performance out of the bag didn't just need to come from the players on the team or even their management team. The hunger needed to come from the terraces as well. They needed to be urging the team on, baying for entertainment, not just warmly applauding acts of fair play and nodding appreciatively when a player exhibited gentlemanly behaviour. Chelsea needed the terraces to be the 12th man.

The League victory in 1954/55 was a phenomenal achievement, particularly given that the team were languishing in 12th position a month before Christmas. In the final match of the season, Chelsea were even clapped off the pitch by their opponents Manchester United, then represented by the Busby Babes.

While success wasn't to be repeated during Drake's tenure, the focus on the talent coming through the youth set-up gave Chelsea the bedrock on which to build their 1960s success.

The Blues saw out the rest of the 1950s with an average league position of 14th, but the team and the fans had at last had a taste of success, and the changes that Drake introduced stuck. What team in the world would be better placed to embrace the swinging sixties?

★ RON HARRIS ★

Ronald Harris was a Hackney-born defender with a robust style of playing. They called him 'Chopper'. He was from Hack knee.

He'd risen though the ranks of the Chelsea Juniors, helping them win the 1960/61 FA Youth Cup before claiming his place in the Blues' First 11 in 1962/63, and was involved in bouncing them straight back into the First Division after relegation in 1961/62. He held a place in the first team for the next 18 years, making a total of 795 appearances and sticking with Chelsea through the relegations and financial challenges of the 1960s and 1970s.

They called him competitive. They called him uncompromising. There's little doubt, though, that he was a man of some considerable talent and commitment. He literally had a strategy for every type of attack. Mostly it was slide-tackles, but he was an exceptional exponent of the skill and generally he got most of the ball.

People knew what to expect when they were facing Chelsea and Chopper was in the back line. His former teammate-turned-adversary Jimmy Greaves, a man who holds several goal-scoring records at the top level of football, only managed to score once against Chelsea when Chopper was holding the back line. The former Tottenham striker once emerged from surgery suggesting he'd had his Ron Harris Memorial Knee replaced.

If Chopper had been as dirty as his reputation, though, then even in those days he would have had more than one red card. But that's all he got. Eighteen years (mostly) at the top of the game and only one red card. And that was rescinded on appeal. Apparently as a result of a witness statement from a vicar. Chopper was virtually an angel.

Harris left Chelsea in 1980 to become player-coach at Brentford, and then player-manager at Aldershot, but retained strong links back to Stamford Bridge (although these were said to be somewhat strained during Ken Bates' tenure as chairman in the 1980s and 1990s).

His list of honours is impressive, winning the European Cup Winners' Cup in 1970/71, the FA Cup in 1969/70 and the Football League Cup in 1964/65. He also made the most appearances for Chelsea in all competitions (795), the most league appearances (655) and the most FA Cup appearances (64).

His brother, Allan Harris, played alongside him for a time, making 70 appearances for Chelsea between 1960 and

1964, before heading off to join other teams. Ultimately, he went into management, taking Queens Park Rangers into the First Division in 1982/83 before jetting off to FC Barcelona and helping them win La Liga (in 1984/85) and taking them to the final of the European Cup (in 1986).

CHELSEA ARE THE FIRST ENGLISH CLUB TO WIN ALL FOUR MAJOR EUROPEAN TITLES, TAKING THE EUROPEAN CUP WINNERS' CUP IN 1971 (AGAINST REAL MADRID), UEFA CHAMPIONS LEAGUE, UEFA EUROPA LEAGUE AND UEFA SUPER CUP.

WE ARE GOING TO
⋆ NEED A BIGGER BUS ⋆

The rules of association football have evolved considerably since they were originally conceived, with one of the biggest changes coming from the size of the pitch.

While there has always been a certain amount of leeway in the size of a football pitch, when the rules of football were originally written down, pitches were originally allowed to be up to 183 metres (200 yards, for those of you who ignored decimalisation half a century ago), which is nearly a third larger than the current size of between 90 and 120 metres (100–130 yards).

The full reason pitches were allowed to be so big is lost to history, but it seems likely to have its roots in the way that association football developed from a village game. There were lots of different ways that the game was played, back in days of yore, but some of them were played over large areas – sometimes, literally between two villages.

This is corroborated by what is generally accepted to be the first formal game of football, played according to Sheffield Rules on Boxing Day in 1860 between Sheffield FC and neighbouring Hallam FC. (Football Association rules were agreed in Woolwich in 1863, but Sheffield didn't take to them until 1877, presumably on the grounds that they were both new-fangled and soft-southern.) The point is, though, that each team fielded 16 players, meaning that they would have needed significantly more space to express their silky Victorian footballing skills.

Pitch size was reduced fairly quickly as football became more formalised, but given the challenges that have faced anyone trying to extend Stamford Bridge, it's hard to imagine how the club could have been able to sustain themselves if they'd needed to buy the land necessary for a pitch that needed to be a third bigger. Where would they have put the executive boxes? Land prices are probably the one thing that would make you want to relocate to the desolate north.

· CHELSEA ·

Player	Club
Bryan Robson	West Bromwich Albion, Manchester United, Middlesborough
Billy Wright	Wolverhampton Wanderers
Frank Lampard	West Ham, Chelsea, Manchester City
Bobby Charlton	Manchester United
Ashley Cole	Arsenal, Chelsea, Derby County
Bobby Moore	West Ham, Fulham
Steven Gerrard	Liverpool
David Beckham	Manchester United
Wayne Rooney	Everton, Manchester United, Derby County
Peter Shilton	Leicester City, Stoke City, Nottingham Forest, Southampton, Derby County, Plymouth Argyle, Wimbledon, Bolton Wanderers, Coventry City, West Ham United, Leyton Orient

Caps

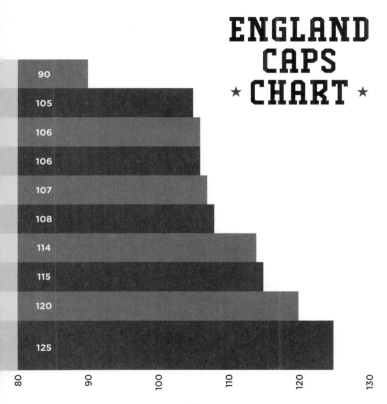

ENGLAND CAPS
★ CHART ★

90
105
106
106
107
108
114
115
120
125

80 90 100 110 120 130

★ RAY WILKINS ★

Ray Wilkins had football in his blood. His father was a professional footballer and so were his three brothers, one of whom played with him at Chelsea. He joined the Blues as an apprentice, making his first team debut as a 17-year-old substitute in 1973.

Two years later, the club was relegated and in financial difficulties as a result of the enhancements to Stamford Bridge, which led to a clear-out of the senior squad and Wilkins being handed the captain's armband. He led the team back into the First Division in 1976/77 and helped them achieve a mid-table finish the following season, but a further relegation in 1978/79 led to him moving on to pastures new. He made 179 league appearances for Chelsea and was also an important figure in the England set-up of the period, making 83 appearances and captaining the Three Lions 10 times.

He moved into management as his playing career came to an end, enjoying two spells as an assistant at Chelsea.

THE OPPOSITION:
★ LEEDS UNITED ★

England, like most countries, has several us vs them splits, but the fault line (traditionally said to be around the Watford Gap services on the M1) between the gritty north and the pampered south is one of the most divisive. East/west has nothing on north/south. And if ever there were two teams that epitomised their respective geographically based stereotypes it would be soft, southern Chelsea and gritty, northern Leeds.

The greatest rivalries in football tend to be forged when two teams of similar stature have a five-or-so-year period when they regularly get in each other's way. Even when those days have passed and teams become leagues apart, the terraces have long memories. It only takes a cup run or a period in the same league to reignite the rivalry.

That's certainly the case with Chelsea and Leeds, who have had issues with one another based on a couple of, to be fair, tasty clashes back in the 1960s and early 1970s. Both teams had vocal, ambitious leaders, with Tommy Docherty keen to put Chelsea where they belonged and Don Revie in the process of making Leeds a force in English football for the first time.

The nature of football means that nobody stays at the top for very long, and both Chelsea and Leeds struggled for silverware as the 1970s turned into the 1980s. As a result, they didn't meet as often in cup runs as time went on, but when they did meet, both teams had notorious firms of hooligans that brought the game into disrepute during this time.

By the 1990s, both teams enjoyed a renaissance, bringing their mutual intolerance back to top-flight football. While all-seater stadiums and CCTV meant that hooliganism off the pitch became less of a problem, matches between Chelsea and Leeds continued to be colourful affairs – with the colours involved often including red and yellow.

The improvement in Chelsea's fortunes in 2003 with Abramovich's arrival coincided with a decline for Leeds; at one point, the two teams didn't meet each other in the league for nearly two decades, but Leeds fans still gave their distain full voice on their first meeting. Chelsea fans initially seemed surprised, presumably because they'd kind of forgotten that Leeds were a thing, but they rose to the occasion and the two teams' fans sang lovely songs to each other as they became reacquainted.

IN THE 1910S, CHELSEA BECAME THE FIRST CLUB IN ENGLAND WITH AN AVERAGE ATTENDANCE OF 40,000.

"I AM HERE TO WIN TROPHIES, YOU KNOW, TO HELP THE TEAM TO REACH OUR TARGETS. I FEEL BLESSED TO HAVE THE OPPORTUNITY TO BRING MY SMALL THING TO THE BIG MACHINE. YOU KNOW, FOR CHELSEA."

Olivier Giroud.

★ DENNIS WISE ★

Dennis Wise came up through Wimbledon's 'Crazy Gang' (via a brief stint in Sweden), joining Chelsea in 1990, becoming captain in 1993 and staying until 2001. During that time, he made 332 league appearances and scored 53 times.

His haul of trophies is impressive, bringing to Stamford Bridge the FA Cup in 1996/97 and 1999/2000, the Football League Cup in 1997/98, the FA Charity Shield in 2000, the UEFA Cup Winners' Cup in 1997/98 and the UEFA Super Cup in 1998.

Wise was an exceptionally committed player but attracted quite a lot of attention from the referee and other authorities. This may have been why he was often overlooked when it came to selection for the national squad, enjoying only 21 caps, but he was very popular on the terraces throughout his career.

In a sign of how inflation was starting to work at the top of the footballing pyramid, Wise signed for Chelsea in 1990 at the age of 25 for a fee that was said to be £1.6 million. Ten years later, at 35, he was sold to Leicester for the same amount.

★ RUUD GULLIT ★

Ruud Gullit was signed by Chelsea in 1995, during Glenn Hoddle's reign – right at the point that the Premier League was settling into its stride and Cool Britannia was becoming a thing. What better time and what better team could there be for an expressive, imaginative player who could apply his skills to virtually any position on the field?

He joined Chelsea as Hoddle was attempting to break down the traditional English 4-4-2 formation, and he brought a level of finesse, freedom and vision to the club that quickly made him popular across the English game (at least with the neutrals).

Within a season of joining the club, he became player-manager, leading Chelsea to glory in the FA Cup, their first trophy in more than a quarter of a century. He promised sexy football and that's what his team provided. He moved on fairly quickly after that, though, with the club and manager allegedly unable to find contractual common ground.

Gullit also played 66 times for the Netherlands, scoring 17 times. He made his debut in 1981 and played a pivotal role in the team wining Euro 88.

EVERYTHING THAT'S WRONG WITH ★ FOOTBALL TODAY ★

In the main, progress is a positive thing and, most of the time, anyone that says things were better in the old days can easily be proved wrong.

DID YOUR MUM KNIT THAT SNOOD?

For example, there are those who suggest football has become too refined, that it's played by preening prima donnas who have the audacity to wear gloves, base layers and even snoods when it's cold. These people overlook the probability that – back in the day – players were very likely to have been hiding a string vest or two underneath their thick woollen football jerseys.

GET OFF MY LAWN

Some people also bemoan the fact that, at the top level, football these days is played on pitches that are as smooth and level as a snooker table. They miss the claggy, February days when players were wading through mud to chase a ball that was so wet it was virtually leaden. They forget quite how slow the game became during the winter, when the ball didn't roll very far because it was slowed down by puddles and goals were as likely to be scored as a result of a random divot as they were by a sublime piece of skill.

They also overlook how many players were forced to retire early through injury after they'd been on the receiving end of one too many crunching tackles where a blood-and-thunder defender had every right to be "going(ish) for the ball", and the general approach was that no one ever got hurt if they were first into the tackle. The bottom line, though, and it is about the bottom line, is that in a world where your new star striker is costing the club around £7 million per second, it's quite irritating to have them put out for nine months by an enthusiastic tackle.

STOP CHANGING THE RULES

Some people also have a problem with the constant rule changes; that in most years, you will still be having discussions about this year's bright new ideas as the November nights draw in as people try to get their heads around embellishments to a set of rules that should be as simple as possible. Progress is inevitable, though, and when you watch an old game now, you realise, for example, how annoying being able to pass back to the goalie was. Will there ever be a perfect set of rules? Unlikely, but they have to keep trying to get there. Does anyone, apart from Eden Hazard, still complain about the introduction of ball boys?

THE JOY OF SOCKS

Despite sounding slightly like one of the lesser-known Sherlock Holmes short stories, the growing issue of the randomly ripped football socks is a weird one. Over the last few years, increasing numbers of players have been ripping their perfectly good football socks because they say that their calves are too mighty and their blood flow is being constrained by the tight-fitting socks.

These are exceptionally highly paid professionals who probably don't have to worry that the tumble dryer has shrunk their socks. There's a decent chance that they get a new pair of socks for every match. Equally, many of them have direct lines to some fairly large and 'innovative' sporting goods manufacturers, so extra-stretchy socks for big-legged and very well-paid strikers should not be beyond their reach.

OKAY COMPUTER?

Then there's the whole VAR thing, which sometimes seems to work one way, sometimes the other way and sometimes not at all. However, once it's got over its teething troubles, there's a decent chance that it will cut down on injustice on the football field. Injustice at the higher levels of football can end up costing considerable amounts of money, so football's governing bodies need to try everything possible to reduce the likelihood of it happening. And isn't it better that we are moaning about a computer on a Saturday afternoon rather than the ref, because the ref's a person and people have feelings.

While technology can take us away from the principle that the game you watch in the Premier League is virtually the same as the game that's played down the park with your mates, with jumpers for goalposts, the professional game was littered with controversies that could have been sorted out in seconds. Take, for example, Frank Lampard's 2010 World Cup goal against Germany that clearly went over the line but wasn't given. England were 2-1 down at the time and went on to lose 4-1, but if Lampard's equaliser had been given, the game would have had a totally different complexion and England might have made it to the next stage of the trophy.

If this had been in a game that mattered, such as one involving Chelsea, the goal that never was would have been even more notorious (apparently the Germans say something similar about the third goal in the 1966 World Cup final, but nobody really needs to pay them any attention).

So, yes, the socks thing is a little odd, VAR can sometimes seem a little wonky, and you are absolutely entitled to moan about the state of the game if you are so inclined, but, in the main, it's a privilege to watch modern football at the highest levels. If blood, thunder and crunching tackles is the kind of entertainment you want, head down to the lower leagues – they are always on the look out for supporters.

Or, if you have a bit of time free and there's no live football being played in the vicinity, head to the video streaming service of your choice and marvel at the 1970 FA Cup final between Chelsea and Leeds ...

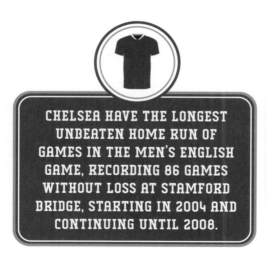

CHELSEA HAVE THE LONGEST UNBEATEN HOME RUN OF GAMES IN THE MEN'S ENGLISH GAME, RECORDING 86 GAMES WITHOUT LOSS AT STAMFORD BRIDGE, STARTING IN 2004 AND CONTINUING UNTIL 2008.

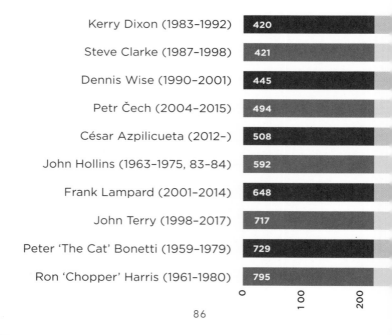

Kerry Dixon (1983–1992) — 420
Steve Clarke (1987–1998) — 421
Dennis Wise (1990–2001) — 445
Petr Čech (2004–2015) — 494
César Azpilicueta (2012–) — 508
John Hollins (1963–1975, 83–84) — 592
Frank Lampard (2001–2014) — 648
John Terry (1998–2017) — 717
Peter 'The Cat' Bonetti (1959–1979) — 729
Ron 'Chopper' Harris (1961–1980) — 795

0   100   200

CHELSEA'S
★ TOP TEN ★
FIRST TEAM
APPEARANCES

(ALL COMPETITIONS)

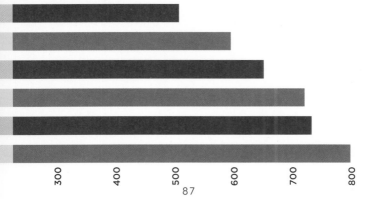

★ GIANFRANCO ZOLA ★

Gianfranco Zola erupted on to the scene in 1996, and has the honour of being described by the then Manchester United manager Alex Ferguson as "a clever little so-and-so", which was pretty much as close to a compliment as any Chelsea player would get from that neck of the woods.

His seven-year career stint with Chelsea brought a kind of cosmopolitan swagger to west London that Gus Mears and his ilk would almost certainly have appreciated. Where Zola differed from those Chelsea buccaneers of old was that he was also an exceptional team player, as capable of setting up goals as he was at finishing them.

Zola was part of the team that won the FA Cup twice in 1996/97 and 1999/2000, the Football League Cup in 1997/98, the FA Charity Shield in 2000, the UEFA Cup Winners' Cup in 1997/98 and the UEFA Super Cup in 1998.

There is a rumour that Zola is in the video for Bonnie Tyler's 'Total Eclipse of the Heart (Turn Around)'. He probably isn't (unless he's one of the inexplicable ninjas).

★ 'LIQUIDATOR' ★

There are several football clubs that have used 'Liquidator' by ska legends the Harry J Allstars as their walk-on tune, including Northampton Town, St Johnstone, West Bromwich Albion, Wolverhampton Wanderers and Wycombe Wanderers, but it tends to be most closely associated with Chelsea. It is Chelsea that are mentioned in the sleeve notes on the band's *Best of …* compilation and, let's face it, the band are probably best placed to know where the royalty cheques come from.

It's a mellow, classy classic and features contributions from musicians that went on to play pivotal roles in both the Wailers (the band that worked with Bob Marley), and the Upsetters (legendary record producer Lee 'Scratch' Perry's house band).

The Blues adopted 'Liquidator' in 1969, perfectly timed for the glorious 1969/70 season that saw Chelsea lift the FA Cup for the first time.

"I DON'T FEEL ANY DIFFERENT TO WHEN I WAS 25, MAYBE BECAUSE I'VE ALWAYS BEEN THIS UNFIT."

Perhaps if Graeme Le Saux had been fitter he wouldn't have been subbed off so often in his first stint at Chelsea.

THE DIRTIEST MATCH ★ IN FOOTBALL ★

The 1970 FA Cup final replay between Chelsea and Leeds has been named the dirtiest match in English football. It would be nice to say that this was because poor weather in Manchester during the days running up to the event had turned Old Trafford, where the replay was held, into a quagmire. It would be nice to say that, but it isn't true.

To set the scene, Chelsea had finished third in the First Division that year, pipped to second by none other than Leeds. In the pre-Champions League world this meant little more than bragging rights, but, in any world where football is played, bragging rights are important.

Equally important was that neither team had won the trophy before, although both had made it to the final within the last decade. This meant that there was real pressure to perform and bring home some silverware, whether to west London or the West Riding of Yorkshire.

The first leg, played at Wembley, had been an inconclusive 2–2 after extra time, so the replay was being played on very tired, grumpy, end-of-the-season legs.

It started out politely enough, but as the game progressed, things seemed to get narkier and narkier. Chelsea, playing in jerseys with a very natty high crew neck, were robust in their tackles, but Leeds gave as good as they got in the early engagements, and it slowly descended into something akin to anarchy.

The words 'scythe', 'crunch', 'headbutt', 'full bodied', 'flying kick', 'melee', 'brawl' and 'ooh, not our Jack' have been associated with the match. Peter Bonetti received an injury to his knee and had to hobble through a fair proportion of the match, although it looks like the magic spray that was thought to be a miracle cure for everything in the 1960s caused more pain than the initial clash.

According to modern analysis, if it was played today, there would have been no fewer than 20 yellow cards and the red card would have been brandished either six or 11 times, depending on who you listen to. It is fair to say that the actual referee, Eric Jennings, who was retiring at the end of the game and clearly thought he was too old for this s**t, let quite a lot slide, only putting Chelsea's Ian Hutchinson in the book.

There were too many incidents that would make a modern audience wince to go into here, but it is fair to say that the match was a fierce contest – with no quarter asked and certainly none given. Chelsea won the day 2–1 after extra time, bringing the FA Cup to Stamford Bridge for the first time.

There have been many hard-fought matches in the history of football, but with a UK TV audience of 28 million, very few have been played quite so publicly.

CHELSEA WERE ONE OF THE FIRST TEAMS TO ADOPT NUMBERED SHIRTS IN 1928, OVER A DECADE BEFORE IT BECAME STANDARD.

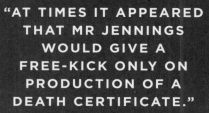

"AT TIMES IT APPEARED THAT MR JENNINGS WOULD GIVE A FREE-KICK ONLY ON PRODUCTION OF A DEATH CERTIFICATE."

Hugh McIlvanney's match report of the 1970 FA Cup final between Chelsea and Leeds United, *the Observer*.

★ GIANLUCA VIALLI ★

Gianluca Vialli joined Chelsea relatively late in his career as part of Ruud Gullit's rebuilding of the team in 1996. He'd already enjoyed a storied career in Italy and, once he reached Chelsea, he quickly became popular on the terraces, although he didn't play often.

Vialli moved seamlessly from player to player-manager, before hanging up his boots entirely so that he could focus on managing the team.

Chelsea were in contention for both the European Cup Winners' Cup and the League Cup when he took over, but he still managed to steer them to the double and deliver a creditable fourth place in the Premier League. His first full season in charge saw the team win the UEFA Super Cup and come in third in the Premier League. But then – as is the nature of things at Stamford Bridge – not long into the next campaign, he was moved on.

He was without a doubt a very cultured chap and, according to legend, he handed out champagne to the players before his first match in charge. From what you can tell of his background, it was probably the good stuff. The club nutritionists presumably wouldn't have allowed it otherwise.

TAKE THE FULHAM ROAD UNTIL YOU ★ REACH THE SHED ★

What came to be called the 'Shed End' was the first major addition to Stamford Bridge, and was added in the 1930s.

Fascinatingly, for all the moaning about the lack of focus on football that sometimes distracted the club as it tried to maintain its champagne lifestyle, it was the Greyhound Racing Association that paid for the development of the southern end of the stadium because they wanted somewhere for their bookies and punters to watch the dog races out of the rain.

The Shed End was originally called the 'Fulham Road End', mostly because, if you look very closely at a map, it backs on to the Fulham Road. It changed its name after pressure from fans in the 1960s coincided with encouragement from the then manager, Tommy Docherty, to bring more atmosphere to home matches. It was felt that while the club could rely on thousands of people to come through the gates on match days, there wasn't an area where die-hard fans could congregate and lead the stadium in song (and sometimes prayer). Chelsea wanted an area like Anfield's Kop, White Hart Lane's Shelf or St James Park's Big Bank.

A letter in the match-day programme in the mid-1960s proposed rechristening the Fulham Road End and making it the focal point for the club's most vociferous fans to come together, and so the Shed End was born. The stand was redeveloped in the mid-1990s, but the name stuck and seems likely to survive no matter how the club redevelops in the future.

THE OPPOSITION: ★ TOTTENHAM HOTSPUR ★

The basis of the real beef between Chelsea and Tottenham dates back to the 1967 FA Cup final. This was the first time that two London teams had met in the final of the cup – and it became known as the 'Cockney Cup Final'.

This is weird because Chelsea are straight out of west London, Tottenham come from north London and

Cockneys are from the east of London, born within the sound of the bells of the church at Bow, as they say. They include people like Ray Winstone, Danny Dyer and Dick Van Dyke. So basically, while plenty of cockneys have played for both teams down the years, neither Chelsea or Tottenham are cockney teams.

But anyway, more than 100,000 people are said to have attended the 1967 FA Cup final, and while the game wasn't particularly contentious (Spurs won 2–1), it is said to have been the start of the fans needling each other. By the end of the 1974/75 season, with the teams locked into a bitter relegation battle, the emerging hooligan culture started to make its presence felt, with a pitch invasion at Stamford Bridge delaying the start of a crucial match between the two that ended with a Spurs victory and Chelsea ultimately dropping a league. Matches between the pair have tended to have a fairly decent amount of spice ever since.

While it is traditional to point out Chelsea's spending power since 2003 and suggest it has tended to prove decisive since the dawn of the new millennium, the Blues' record against Tottenham in the Premier League as a whole is seriously impressive.

Let's start with the simple stuff. There have been on average around 2.75 Premier League goals per meeting between the pair, with only 12% of matches sagging to a 0-0. That's pretty much in line with clashes between the League's larger clubs.

Where it gets interesting, though, is the fact that Chelsea's first Premier League loss to Tottenham was in 2006, nearly a decade and a half after the League was formed. But it doesn't stop there. In the 60 times the pair have faced each other between the creation of the new league and the conclusion of the 2021/22 season, Chelsea have only lost 12% of the time. That's seven games out of 60 against Spurs. If you split that out into home and away matches, Chelsea have lost 20% of matches at either White Hart Lane or the Tottenham Hotspur Stadium, but they've only lost 3% of matches at Stamford Bridge.

If you really want to be technical about it, Chelsea's Premier League record against Tottenham has actually deteriorated since 2003, going from winning 60% of the time to just over half the time. Chelsea have lost around 20% of matches against Spurs since 2003, but prior to 2003, the percentage was zero. Doughnuts. Zip. None.

Football is always about the future, the next competition, the next trophy. But that's still pretty impressive.

CHELSEA ARE ONE OF ONLY THREE MAJOR FOOTBALL CLUBS TO HAVE PLAYED IN THE SAME STADIUM SINCE THEY WERE SET UP. THE OTHERS ARE LIVERPOOL AND SHEFFIELD UNITED.

★ FRANK LEBOEUF ★

Frank Leboeuf was one of an influx of players that arrived to help Chelsea with their inexorable rise in the mid-1990s. Marseille-born, the centre-back came up through the French lower leagues before joining Strasbourg and then making the leap to Chelsea in 1996.

He made 204 appearances for the Blues between 1996 and 2001, making a regular contribution at both ends of the pitch with set pieces and penalties alongside his defensive duties. He helped Chelsea win the FA Cup in 1996/97 and 1999/2000 (the last one played at the old Wembley), the Football League Cup in 1997/98, the FA Charity Shield in 2000, the UEFA Cup Winners' Cup in 1997/98 and the UEFA Super Cup in 1998.

He was also capped more than 50 times for France, winning the FIFA World Cup in 1998, the UEFA European Championship in 2000 and the FIFA Confederations Cup in 2001.

Frank is now enjoying an unlikely second career as an actor and producer, appearing in 15 TV series and films to date, including starring alongside Eddie Redmayne in *The Theory of Everything*. It's a speaking part, so it's more than most of us have achieved.

THE BATTLE OF STAMFORD BRIDGE ★ (2016) ★

If we are being honest, it's not impossible that some football matches aren't actually all that memorable. The matches, for example, that are played on drizzly February Tuesday evenings, where the stakes are relatively low for both teams and there's a risk that the price of the half-time pint is more interesting than what's happening on the pitch.

Then there are the other kind of matches. The matches where seasons and reputations are on the line. Sometimes it's not even your season.

The 2015/16 season was reaching its climax, with surprise package Leicester in the box seat. Tottenham were still in with a chance of catching them, but had squandered two points the week before by giving away the lead at West Bromwich Albion.

Standing between them and the three points that they so desperately needed was Chelsea, champions in 2014/15. Tottenham had not won at Stamford Bridge since 1990 but Chelsea's season had been, with the best will in the world, middling.

Football is a game of 90 minutes, of 22 players, their management and a handful of officials. What happens on the pitch is most of the game ... but not all of it. John Terry and some of the other Chelsea team had spent the week quietly winding up the Spurs team in the media, raising the stakes and adding to their tension.

You wouldn't have guessed that as half-time approached, though. Tottenham had gone about their business, with Harry Kane and Heung-Min Son tucking home what might grudgingly be called a nice couple of goals. There had been a couple of yellow cards brandished in Tottenham's direction, but nothing particularly untoward.

Then, just before the break it kicked off in a big way. A late challenge by Danny Rose led to an altercation, which descended into a brawl. Two more yellow cards were shown, the very least that was deserved.

The pressure had clearly got to Tottenham and eight more yellow cards were shown during the second half. Importantly two goals from Gary Cahill and Eden Hazard levelled the match, so Spurs dropped two more points and the title moved beyond them. There was a further brawl at the end. Both teams received hefty fines and the match was immortalised as 'the Battle of Stamford Bridge'.

It was definitely the other kind of match.

CHELSEA'S 21-0 VICTORY OVER LUXEMBOURG'S JEUNESSE HAUTCHARAGE IN THE UEFA CUP WINNERS' CUP IN 1971 REMAINS A RECORD IN EUROPEAN COMPETITION.

"I ALLOWED THEM TO SELF-DESTRUCT SO ALL THE MEDIA, ALL THE PEOPLE IN THE WORLD, WENT 'TOTTENHAM LOST THE TITLE.'"

Referee Mark Clattenburg avoiding any blame in Spurs throwing away the league during the Battle of Stamford Bridge.

Player	Club
Michael Owen	Liverpool, Newcastle United, Manchester United, Stoke City
Jermain Defoe	Bournemouth, Sunderland, Tottenham Hotspur, Portsmouth, West Ham, Charlton Athletic
Robbie Fowler	Liverpool, Leeds, Manchester City, Blackburn Rovers
Thierry Henry	Arsenal
Frank Lampard	West Ham, Chelsea, Manchester City
Sergio Agüero	Manchester City
Andrew Cole	Sunderland, Portsmouth, Manchester City, Fulham, Blackburn Rovers, Manchester United, Newcastle United
Wayne Rooney	Everton, Manchester United
Harry Kane	Tottenham Hotspur
Alan Shearer	Blackburn Rovers, Newcastle United

Goa

PREMIER LEAGUE'S
★ TOP SCORERS ★

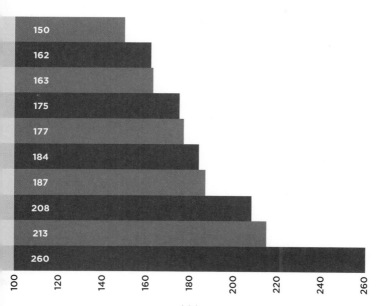

★ RAISING THE ROOF ★

In a lot of ways, the large audiences that Chelsea could attract meant that the club was relatively relaxed about adding more terraces and luxuries such as roofing. The North Stand gained a roof shortly after the war, and then it was another 20 years before the West Stand was redeveloped.

While there were plans to completely redevelop the stadium in the 1960s, nothing came of them. By the 1970s, though, the East Stand was nigh-on 60-years-old and redevelopment became a priority.

With Archibald Leitch no longer available, Chelsea decided to hire architects that had never worked on football stadiums before. Sometimes decisions like that can be brave, sometimes they can be foolhardy. In Chelsea's case, it was the latter. What was described as one of the most ambitious building projects ever undertaken in Britain was soon mired in crisis.

It was the 1970s, so there were strikes. The availability of materials dried up and costs ballooned. Chelsea quickly found themselves in debt to the tune of around £4 million, so they had no money for new players. There was also frequent trouble on the terraces and little success on the pitch since the turn of the decade. At the same time, Britain was going through a very challenging time economically. Gate receipts fell, and Chelsea's fortunes started to spiral. The team dropped down to the Second Division at the end of the 1974/75 and 1978/79 seasons, and bankruptcy started to look like a very real possibility.

One of the ways that Chelsea tried to keep afloat was selling the freehold for the ground; this was a move that would have significant repercussions in the years to come.

CHELSEA WERE THE FIRST TEAM TO WIN THE FA CUP AT THE NEW WEMBLEY STADIUM IN 2007.

★ CLAUDE MAKÉLÉLÉ ★

Part of what makes football such an entertaining game is that a successful team needs 11 people on the pitch doing lots of different things. And, as Chelsea know from bitter experience, if everyone is going for personal glory all the time, there's a decent chance that you will get caught on the counter-attack.

Claude Makélélé offered something different, providing generous midfield support that let more attack-minded players push forward. He saw his role as someone the team could rely on to break up the counter-attack and generally stop the opposition if it looked like they were starting to get ambitious.

He signed for Chelsea from Real Madrid in 2003 and spent the next five years providing a solid, unflashy shield for the defence, making plays for the team as it went on its successful hunt for glory.

He made 217 appearances for Chelsea in all competitions, and was a pivotal part of the team that won four English trophies and the Premier League twice. He's that rarest of things: a midfield legend that only scored twice.

★ A KICK UP THE 1980S ★

By the mid-1980s, Chelsea were in dire straits. The fair-weather fans and celebrity guests were evaporating as quickly as the team's performances, and in 1982/83 Chelsea faced the very real prospect of a drop into the English third tier, only narrowly escaping by two points.

By the next season, though, things were starting to stabilise and the club got back to the top flight – where they belonged – as champions of the Second Division. Two creditable and consecutive sixth places in the First Division gave the fans some anticipation of a return to the glory days, but 14th place in 1986/87 gave way to relegation in 1987/88 and then a swift return as champions the next year. These were testing times.

It was fractious off the pitch as well, with crowd trouble leading to the chairman having electric fences put up around the stadium to stop clashes between opposing fans and pitch invasions. They were never switched on (it turns out the FA, the Greater London Council and the United Nations were dubious about such things), but they were a very visible example of the trouble that the club found itself in.

The 1990s started more brightly, with Chelsea enjoying fifth place in 1989/90, and then sagging to 11th in 1990/91 and 14th in the final season before the Premier League era commenced.

CHELSEA BROUGHT THE FIRST NON-BRITISH PLAYER TO THE ENGLISH LEAGUES IN 1913 (SEE PAGE 26) AND WERE THE FIRST ENGLISH SIDE TO FIELD AN ENTIRELY NON-BRITISH TEAM IN 1999 AGAINST SOUTHAMPTON.

★ DIDIER DROGBA ★

During a time of phenomenal success on the field, Didier Drogba stands with a small handful of his teammates that have a long list of personal awards to go alongside the team trophies.

He was fast, he was strong, and there's a decent chance that more than a few defenders of the time are still waking up in terror at the thought of trying to stand between him and the goal. He is fourth on the list of Chelsea's all-time goal scorers for a very good reason: there are very few better.

In his first two years at Chelsea, he helped deliver consecutive Premier League titles, doubling the number of top-flight trophies that the Blues had won in a century.

There is not enough space in this book to list his personal honours, but as part of the Chelsea team, he won the Premier League in 2004/05, 2005/06, 2009/10 and 2014/15, the FA Cup in 2006/07, 2008/09, 2009/10 and 2011/12, the Football League Cup in 2004/05, 2006/07 and 2014/15, the FA Community Shield in 2005 and 2009, and the UEFA Champions League in 2011/12. Which is not bad for someone who didn't sign a professional contract until he was 21.

RESPECT THE BADGE: A LION IN THE 1980S ★ AND 1990S ★

There was a dawning realisation among several football clubs as the 1980s went on that there was a possibility they didn't really know exactly where the documents were that proved they owned the copyright to their logos. A bit like car tax, they knew they'd put the documents in that box in the cupboard under the stairs at some point in the 1950s, but when they came to look for them three decades later, they simply couldn't find them.

This was a problem because, as football culture evolved in the 1980s, clubs were making more and more money from replica kits and merchandise. Enforcing copyright was challenging when they couldn't prove they owned the intellectual property.

By the 1980s, the club was in financial difficulties and they really had to make sure that every revenue stream was locked down.

At the same time, the arrival of Ken Bates as club chairman meant that it was a great opportunity to make a change to their image.

And so the decision was made to change the club badge, moving from the heraldic badge of yore to a brave new badge that brought together both the lion and the 'CFC' that had been the logo for a single season back in the 1950s.

A lot of people are instinctively resistant to change, particularly when it comes to football, which can be the bedrock of many lives, so any time that a logo evolves or changes there tends to be what is technically called 'pushback'. This was easier to deal with in the days before social media, because if you were, let's say, a football team, you could simply ignore the sackloads of post from irritated fans who objected to the new logo and there was less of a forum where a move against a change could gather pace.

The widely voiced complaint about the Chelsea logo in the 1980s and 1990s is that it sails a little too close to the lion that graces the Millwall FC logo. As a result, when the new millennium rolled around and Ken Bates brought his ownership of Chelsea FC to an end in 2004, fan pressure – and the approaching centenary of the club – led to the reintroduction of the classic 1950s badge, slightly updated to reflect the fashions of the age. One assumes that this time they have kept hold of the copyright information.

SERIAL BALLON D'OR WINNER LIONEL MESSI HAS PLAYED SEVEN MATCHES AGAINST CHELSEA BUT NEVER SCORED. HE EVEN MISSED A PENALTY AGAINST THEM AT THE NOU CAMP IN 2012.

"I NEVER MAKE FORECASTS, BUT WHOEVER WINS THAT GAME WILL WIN THE FINAL."

Ken Bates unexpectedly does a thing that he said he wasn't going to do ...

123

THIS USED TO BE A FOOTBALL PITCH, ★ YOU KNOW ★

Off the pitch, drama continued to be the order of the day, though. The club had been purchased for £1 in the early 1980s, but the Mears family had kept hold of the freehold for the ground. They subsequently sold this to a property development company, who quickly decided that they would make more money by redeveloping the stadium as housing or perhaps a supermarket.

These developers also owned Fulham – and subsequently added Queens Park Rangers (QPR) to their portfolios. They proved their absolute commitment to football and their understanding of the local community by proposing to merge Fulham and QPR so they could sell off Craven Cottage for executive riverside flats.

This meant that from around the middle of the 1980s, the

Chelsea fans and club leadership were forced to focus virtually all of their time and resources not on the action on the pitch, but on actually saving the pitch. In 1986, the 'Save the Bridge' appeal was launched to support the long and expensive legal battle that ran until 1992, when the property developers very sadly found themselves on the wrong end of the free market. The property market collapsed and they were, unfortunately, forced into bankruptcy. It's amazing how much sympathy they didn't get.

The freehold was returned to Chelsea, and while it is still operated under a different structure to the football club, it seems that there are sufficient controls in place to stop a similar situation ever arising again.

★ PETR ČECH ★

Petr Čech is one of the greatest goalkeepers, certainly in Premier League history, if not the entire history of football. He signed for Chelsea from Rennes in 2004 and went on to make 333 league appearances and 494 total appearances for the Blues. He also surpassed Peter Bonetti's clean sheet record.

He helped Chelsea win 15 major trophies during his time with the Blues – four Premier League titles in 2004/05, 2005/06, 2009/10 and 2014/15, the FA Cup four times in 2006/07, 2008/09, 2009/10 and 2011/12, the Football League Cup three times in 2004/05, 2006/07, 2014/15, the FA Community Shield twice in 2005 and 2009, the UEFA Champions League in 2011/12 and the Europa League in 2012/13.

He also enjoyed an impressive international career with the Czech Republic, receiving 124 caps.

Having put his playing days behind him, Čech now plays ice hockey in Division 1 of the English league. The goal's smaller but it's not necessarily what you'd call a safe retirement.

PREMIER LEAGUE ATTENDANCES:
★ CHELSEA ★

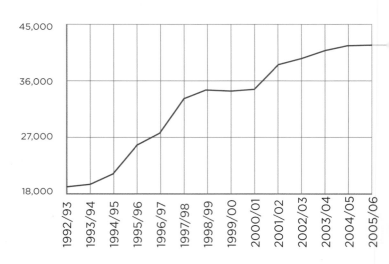

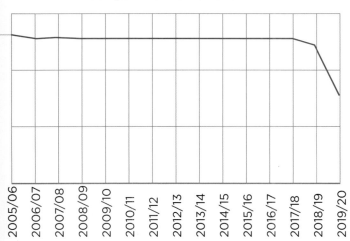

Note: Data post 2018/19 does not compare due to Covid-19.

FRESH INVESTMENT ★ AND NEW STARTS ★

While the legal issues were fading into the background, the Blues were a long way from being on a secure financial footing, and so Chelsea's chairman put out a request for new investment. Up stepped Matthew Harding, who had worked his way up from the tea room to the board rooms of the insurance industry, amassing a healthy fortune in the process.

As a lifelong Chelsea supporter, he invested a considerable amount in the club, helping fund the change in fortunes that were witnessed as the top flight of English football transmogrified from the First Division to the Premier League. His investment helped the club move ahead with a redevelopment of the North Stand, which was renamed the 'Matthew Harding Stand' after he tragically lost his life in a helicopter crash while travelling back from a Chelsea match.

On the pitch, results reflected what was going on around Stamford Bridge. Things were uncertain as the Premier League got going, with Chelsea stuttering to 11th, 14th, 11th, another 11th ... But then, in 1996/97, the Blues cracked the top six and have never looked back (all right, they've looked back once, in 2015/16, but that's still a quarter of a century with no worse than 10th).

This consistency has been driven by the team getting all of its ducks in a row, as they say. The chairmen have been basically understanding and willing to invest in the team, the stadium was completely overhauled in the 1990s and offers an excellent match-day experience, and the teams on the pitch have been a good combination of established global superstars and a string of superb youngsters that have come through the Academy.

There is still drama, there are good years and bad, but 30 years ago, 10th place in the top flight would have been an achievement. Over the last 20 years, the Blues have delivered an average league position of third, and have only missed out on Champion's League qualification three times.

Chelsea have earned their place as one of the best teams in the world.

★ FRANK LAMPARD ★

Frank Lampard was one of Chelsea's most loyal team members, holding a place in the team for 13 years as a midfield lynchpin in a period of unprecedented success. He scored the winning goal in 2004/05 that confirmed Chelsea's first Premier League title and the club's first top-flight victory since 1954/55, and has a host of other honours associated with his name, including the most consecutive Premier League appearances.

Lampard joined Chelsea in 2001 from West Ham United (and a short loan to Swansea) and quickly developed into an exceptional midfield player, working hard to constantly enhance his game. He soon became a favourite on the terraces, with an exceptional work rate, a keen eye for a pass and, most importantly, being someone who seemed to clearly enjoy being there.

It's fair to say that Lampard had a glittering career, winning the Premier League in 2004/05, 2005/06 and 2009/10, the FA Cup in 2006/07, 2008/09, 2009/10 and 2011/12, the Football League Cup in 2004/05 and 2006/07, the FA Community Shield in 2005 and 2009, the UEFA Champions League in 2011–12 and the UEFA Europa League in 2012–13. One of the few achievements in domestic football that eluded him was promotion from the

Second Division, but it's fair to say that – all in all – he did okay.

He was also a stalwart of the England team, and is currently the joint seventh most-capped England player alongside Bobby Charlton. He was capped for the first time in 1999, but didn't play at a major tournament until Euro 2004, where he scored against both France and Croatia in the group stages. He went on to captain the side regularly and thumped in 29 goals in his 106 appearances before retiring from international football in 2014.

After his playing days, he went into management – with varying degrees of success – and also published a series of books for children.

STAMFORD BRIDGE IS TECHNICALLY IN FULHAM, NOT CHELSEA. LONDON'S WEIRD LIKE THAT.

"LAMPS IS LAMPS. WHEN HE PLAYS WELL HE IS BEST IN THE GAME. WHEN HE PLAYS BAD, HE IS THE SECOND OR THIRD BEST."

Roy Keane doesn't give praise often, so you know he means it.

PREMIER LEAGUE
★ MANAGERS' TIMELINE ★

Up to the end of the 2021/22 season, Chelsea have employed the services of 20 managers during the Premier League years, including two that have returned for a second bite of the cherry after they had initially moved on.

On average they stay for around 18 months, which is a similar sort of length as a Tottenham manager, and to be fair, it is often Tottenham that pick them up after Chelsea have finished with them (four times). The 18 months includes caretaker managers who stick around for a few months to help the team finish a season and, as a result, bring the average down a bit.

Ultimately, most management careers end in failure, and while Chelsea have a reputation for a lack of patience when it comes to managers, they don't appear to be much more brutal than other teams. Managers have around a season and a transfer window to make their mark on the team. Some do, some don't.

Season	Month	Manager
1992/93	August 1992	Ian Porterfield
1992/93	February 1993	David Webb
1992/93	June 1993	Glenn Hoddle
1995/96	May 1996	Ruud Gullit
1997/98	February 1998	Gianluca Vialli
2000/01	September 2000	Claudio Ranieri
2003/04	June 2004	José Mourinho
2007/08	September 2007	Avram Grant
2007/08	July 2008	Luiz Felipe Scolari
2008/09	February 2009	Guus Hiddink
2008/09	July 2009	Carlo Ancelotti
2010/11	June 2011	André Villas-Boas
2011/12	March 2012	Roberto Di Matteo
2012/13	November 2012	Rafael Benítez
2013/14	June 2013	José Mourinho (2)
2015/16	December 2015	Guus Hiddink (2)
2015/16	July 2016	Antonio Conte
2018/19	July 2018	Maurizio Sarri
2018/19	July 2019	Frank Lampard
2020/21	January 2021	Thomas Tuchel
2022/23	September 2022	Graham Potter
2023	July 2023	Mauricio Pochettino

Season	Player	Goals
2002/03	Gianfranco Zola	14
2003/04	Jimmy Floyd Hasselbaink	12
2004/05	Frank Lampard	13
2005/06	Frank Lampard	16
2006/07	Didier Drogba	20
2007/08	Frank Lampard	10
2008/09	Nicolas Anelka	19
2009/10	Didier Drogba	29
2010/11	Florent Malouda	13
2011/12	Frank Lampard/Daniel Sturridge	11
2012/13	Frank Lampard	15
2013/14	Eden Hazard	14
2014/15	Diego Costa	20
2015/16	Diego Costa	12
2016/17	Diego Costa	20
2017/18	Eden Hazard	12
2018/19	Eden Hazard	16
2019/20	Tammy Abraham	15
2020/21	Jorginho	7
2021/22	Masoount	11
2022/23	Raheem Sterling	10

CHELSEA'S LEADING GOAL SCORERS
★ BY SEASON ★
(PREMIER LEAGUE)

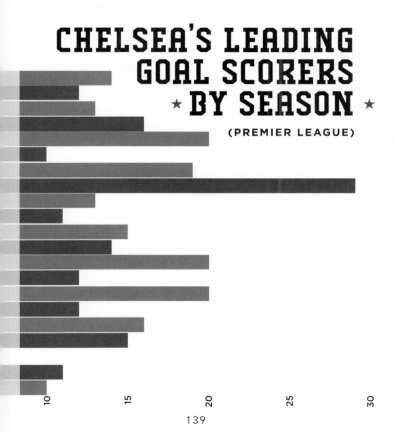

★ JOHN TERRY ★

John Terry held the line for Chelsea as a central defender 492 times. He was the first captain to lift the FA Cup at the new Wembley stadium and is Chelsea's most successful captain.

He started out at West Ham United as a midfielder before moving into Chelsea's youth team at 14, slowly evolving into the defensive role for which he later became famous. He started making regular appearances in the first team in the 2000/01 season before taking the captain's armband for the first time in December 2001. Terry became club captain when José Mourinho arrived in the 2003/04 season, going on to play the role in more than 500 matches.

He was also captain of England, succeeding David Beckham. He played 78 times for the Three Lions and was the first senior player to score at England's new Wembley home.

Terry is the president of Chelsea FC Women and has been an active advocate of the women's game.

THE OPPOSITION:
★ ARSENAL ★

Chelsea are blessed with several local teams nearby, some of whom sometimes have the ability to play football to quite a high level ... but since the Premier League came along, there is only one that has consistently been worthy of consideration as a rival.

Matches between Chelsea and Arsenal have always been worth watching, with an average of three goals per match and only six 0–0 draws in the 60 times that the two teams have met since the inception of the Premier League.

It's a rivalry that has thrown up some fascinating encounters and some entertaining results, including the time that Chelsea beat Arsenal 6–0 as the Gunners looked to celebrate Arsène Wenger's 1,000th game in charge.

Several players have moved from north to west London, and one or two of them have played for Arsenal and then managed Chelsea and vice versa. While there have been some tensions when someone's moved between the two clubs, these have tended to be the result of specific circumstances rather than ongoing issues between them.

There has been a shift in the balance of power since 2003, with Chelsea now winning 44% of the time, as opposed to 14% of the time, and the proportion of draws falling from around 33% to around 26% over the same period.

Weirdly enough, it was Arsenal that finally got celery banned from Stamford Bridge after a few of their players had the vegetable thrown at them in 2007. The celery thing had been a tradition for at least a couple of decades and was based on the sort of song that you really shouldn't sing in public. After a couple of Arsenal players were pelted with celery during a match in 2007, the FA launched an inquiry. Celery is now explicitly on the list of banned substances at Stamford Bridge, so Chelsea fans have had to change their mid-match snack of choice because of Arsenal, but Chelsea still don't particularly bear them any ill-will. It's probably because for most of the last 20 years, Chelsea have been simply better.

KEN BATES PURCHASED CHELSEA FOR £1 IN 1982 AND SOLD IT FOR A COOL £140 MILLION IN 2003. NOBODY DARES ASK IF HE MADE A PROFIT.

★ GETTING SHIRTY ★

Arsenal make a big play of the fact that they were the innovators that used shirt numbers for the first time in the top flight of English football, but they tend to ignore two facts.

Firstly, they were playing Sheffield Wednesday, who were also in shirt numbers, so technically they were one of the first two teams that played in shirt numbers.

Secondly, Chelsea also played in shirt numbers on the same day against Swansea Town, so technically Arsenal can give it the big one as much as they like, but really they were one of the first four teams that played in numbered shirts. Which, let's be honest, is less of a flex.

In the interests of fairness, though, it should be pointed out that there were a couple of differences between the two matches. In the case of Chelsea and Swansea, it was only the outfield players that had their shirts numbered – the goalies were presumably in thick, woollen polo jumpers and flat caps that were de rigueur in 1920s football –

while the Arsenal versus Sheffield match numbered all 22 players on the pitch. The other difference between the two matches is that the match between Chelsea and Swansea took place in the Second Division, which doesn't technically qualify as a top flight match, but maybe we can put that in a smaller font or something ...

Ultimately, it's worth pointing out that no matter which team brought the idea into English football in 1928, it wasn't even remotely an original idea. The Australian and New Zealand football teams had been using numbered shirts for international matches since at least 1922. If the historians are to be believed, the practice had been relatively common on the other side of the world since the turn of the 20th century, particularly when it came to state and international games where fans were less likely to recognise opposition players.

Ultimately, it seems that the Australian and New Zealand football teams might even have picked up the idea originally from a niche sport called Rugby Union that was moderately popular in the southern hemisphere at the time, and which was thought to have been numbering shirts since the 1860s.

The bigger question is why it took another couple of decades before numbered shirts were adopted more widely in the English game. The answer appears to be that the majority of football teams did not think that numbering shirts was necessary because the fans that came regularly to matches should be able to recognise their own players. Also, according to discussions at the time, they didn't want their footballers to end up looking like jockeys. Cynics might also suggest that it's not impossible that they didn't want to make life easy for match officials ...

CHELSEA PLAYED THEIR FIRST MATCH USING GOAL-LINE TECHNOLOGY DURING THE 2012 FIFA CLUB WORLD CUP. IT WASN'T NEEDED FOR THE GAME BUT FRANK LAMPARD, WHO FAMOUSLY HAD A GOAL DISALLOWED IN THE 2010 WORLD CUP, WAS RATHER PLEASED.

HENRY VIII:
★ THE GREAT I AM ★

The thing about royalty is that no matter how powerful, no matter how well intentioned, when they move on, they often leave behind a gigantic mess to clean up. And that mess sometimes lingers for hundreds of years and can have an impact in the very strangest of ways.

King Henry VIII reigned from 1509 to 1547, arguably ushering in a golden age for England (not necessarily for the rest of the world, but for England). He changed the relationship between church and state, reformed parliament and provided the tabloid newspapers with a steady stream of fascinating sagas.

He also started the process of turning London into the city that it is today, overseeing the process of bringing Old St Paul's Cathedral to new glory and adding protections to certain parks so that they would always be there for him to hunt.

But that's not all. In Richmond Park, there is a mound, thought to be a Bronze Age burial site, that King Henry VIII is said to like to ride up when he was out hunting so that he could check out the work going on at St Paul's 10 miles (16 km) away in central London. Given that he was all about the divine right of kings, it was probably important to him that he had a good view of one of his primary

149

places for having a natter with God (it is also said that he once went up the mound to receive a signal that the execution Anne Boleyn, AKA wife number two, had been completed).

If there's one thing that's more convoluted than the history of football, it's the history of architecture, but according to laws enacted since his death, this view is protected in perpetuity, so even five and a half centuries later no buildings are allowed to block the view between a mound in TW10 and St Paul's Cathedral in EC4M.

Which is all quirky and entertainingly olde worlde London unless you are trying to redevelop a football stadium that is directly on the sightline between Richmond and St Paul's. Which Stamford Bridge is.

Very few problems are insurmountable, but it does add complication to proposals to redevelop the stadium, and in the building trade, 'complications' is a nice way of saying 'cost'. The most recent plan suggested digging down so that the pitch would be lower than ground level, but that could deliver a whole new set of historical challenges because we know that there's a lot of excavated earth from the creation of the Piccadilly Line down there (see page 17), as well as the ashes of some of the older players. The only thing we know that isn't down there is the remains of the Battle of Stamford Bridge (see page 48).

West London is different to north London, where there's always an old industrial estate you can take over and build on if you are a football club that doesn't mind moving. Chelsea either have to put up with an excellent but perhaps not state-of-the-art stadium, move somewhere new or find a way to accommodate the whims of a 500-year-old regal spectre.

Because Henry VIII is probably pretty high on the list of ghosts you don't want to be haunted by, perhaps the answer is to raise the royal hillock rather than lower the Bridge.

> **CHELSEA'S MATCH-DAY MASCOTS ARE STAMFORD THE LION AND BRIDGET THE LIONESS (WHO ARRIVED IN 2013)**

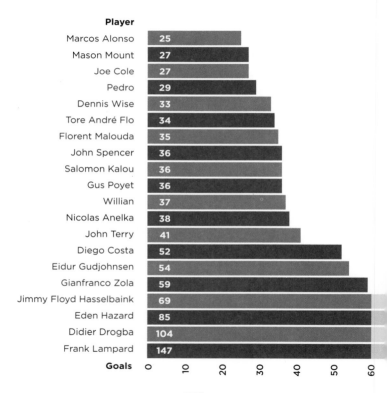

Player	Goals
Marcos Alonso	25
Mason Mount	27
Joe Cole	27
Pedro	29
Dennis Wise	33
Tore André Flo	34
Florent Malouda	35
John Spencer	36
Salomon Kalou	36
Gus Poyet	36
Willian	37
Nicolas Anelka	38
John Terry	41
Diego Costa	52
Eidur Gudjohnsen	54
Gianfranco Zola	59
Jimmy Floyd Hasselbaink	69
Eden Hazard	85
Didier Drogba	104
Frank Lampard	147

CHELSEA'S LEADING PREMIER LEAGUE ★ GOAL SCORERS ★

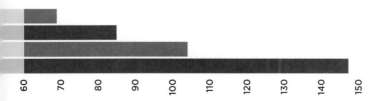

★ CHELSEA FC WOMEN ★

Women's football has had a convoluted journey, with almost as many false dawns as the Chelsea men's team. The success of the Lionesses in Euro 2022 means that it has now established itself as part of the fabric of most major football clubs.

The female game was actually very popular between 1880 and 1920, with some matches attracting solid crowds of around 10,000 and, by all accounts, offering good entertainment, even if they did wear inexplicable bonnets that don't really look like they were much help when it rained.

The FA withdrew its support for the game in 1921, though. They presumably had their reasons, but there's no evidence that they were particularly good reasons on either medical, moral or entertainment grounds.

While there was a short-lived women's team in the 1970s, it was 70 years before Chelsea Ladies Football Club, the direct precursor of Chelsea FC Women, was created in

1992. It formally became part of the Chelsea FC set-up in 2004, at around the same time as the team reached the top flight of the women's football in England.

The Women's Super League (WSL) was formed in 2011 and Chelsea Women have been champions six times in 2015, 2017/18, 2019/20, 2020/21, 2021/22 and 2022/23. They have also won the FA WSL Spring Series in 2017, the Women's FA Cup five times in 2014/15, 2017/18, 2020/21, 2021/22 and 2022/23, the FA Women's League Cup twice in 2019/20 and 2020/21, and the Women's FA Community Shield in 2020 and 2023. They've done the double five times and even the treble once.

While Chelsea's men's team wasted no time in reaching the top division of English football at the start of the 20th century but then waited half a century before delivering any silverware, the Chelsea Women took their time to reach the top flight but have enjoyed glorious success since their arrival.

★ KAREN CARNEY ★

Solihull-born Karen Carney joined Chelsea during the 2015/16 season and stayed until she retired from the pitch at the end of the 2018/19 season. She helped lead the team to a FA Women's Cup/Women's Super League double in 2017/18 as well as securing victory in the WSL Spring Series in 2017. She was also named the club's player of the year in 2016.

Carney played an important role in the England team, making her international debut in 2005. When she retired she was the second most capped England player with 144 appearances, (although Jill Scott has subsequently overtaken her). She took part in four FIFA Women's World Cups in 2007, 2011, 2015 and 2019 and four UEFA Women's Championships in 2005, 2009, 2013 and 2017. She was also part of the team that represented Great Britain at the 2012 Summer Olympics.

Throughout her career she continued to pursue academic qualifications and is currently leading a government review into the future of the women's professional game across the country. Former Chelsea coach Emma Hayes, as well as Arsenal's Ian Wright, are also part of the expert panel that has been providing input into Carney's report.

★ THE GAP ★

The Football League is deceptively clever and fiendishly cruel: a ten-month tournament where teams get three points for a win, one point for a draw and no points for coming second. Every team starts the season in August with hope and optimism, and, in most cases, that hope and optimism is slowly squeezed out of them as autumn turns to winter. By spring, there are usually, realistically, only three or four teams still in it.

For most teams, it can be quite useful (and sobering) to look at the gap between how many points the champions got and how many points the team in question took.

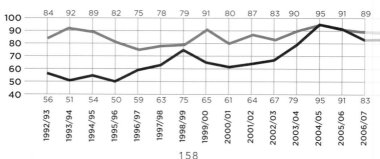

In the case of the Premier League, it's a little more complicated with Chelsea, who enjoyed a period of phenomenal success at the turn of the millennium and have tended, with the best will in the world, to have been a little erratic ever since. So it's not quite such a useful gauge, but it still tells a story.

Over the three decades of the Premier League, Chelsea have been 17 points off the pace in an average season. Despite winning the League twice, the last 10 years have not been quite so successful by this measure: the team have slipped to 21 points behind the champions in an average year. The gap has been 28 points on average over the last five years, although let's be fair here, the gap has never been bigger than it was in 2022/23 and it will never be that big again (hopefully).

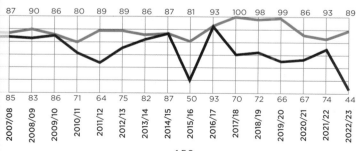

THE
★ TROPHY CABINET ★

Competition	Year
First Division Premier League	1954/55, 2004/05, 2005/06, 2009/10, 2014/15, 2016/17
Second Division	1983/84, 1988/89
FA Cup	1969/70, 1996/97, 1999/2000, 2006/07, 2008/09, 2009/10, 2011/12, 2017/18
Football League Cup EFL Cup	1964/65, 1997/98, 2004/05, 2006/07, 2014/15
FA Charity Shield FA Community Shield	1955, 2000, 2005, 2009
Full Members' Cup	1986, 1990
European Cup UEFA Champions League	2011/12, 2020/21
UEFA Cup UEFA Europa League	2012/13, 2018/19
UEFA Cup Winners' Cup	1970/71, 1997/98
UEFA Super Cup	1998, 2021
FIFA Club World Cup	2021